G. A. BAKER
9 ANDOVER HOUSE
BROADMERE AVENUE,
HAVANT HANTS
PO9 5HY

ANDOVER
TO
SOUTHAMPTON

Vic Mitchell and Keith Smith

MP *Middleton Press*

Cover Picture: The 12.53pm Portsmouth & Southsea to Andover Junction drifts into the oil lit Clatford station on 12th October 1957. The locomotive is class M7 0-4-4T no. 30357, built in 1900. (J.J.Smith)

First published September 1990

ISBN 0 906520 82 7

© Middleton Press 1990

Design and Laser typesetting -
        Deborah Goodridge
        Barbara Mitchell

Published by Middleton Press
        Easebourne Lane
        Midhurst, West Sussex
        GU29 9AZ
        Tel. (0730) 813169

Printed & bound by Biddles Ltd,
        Guildford and Kings Lynn

CONTENTS

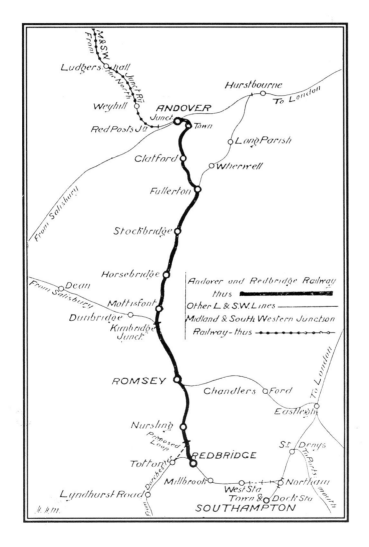

Map from the January 1910 Railway Magazine, showing a loop near Redbridge which was authorised in 1906 but never built.

ACKNOWLEDGEMENTS

We are grateful for the help received from many of the photographers mentioned in the captions and also from R.M.Casserley, C.R.L.Coles, Dr.E.Course, G.Croughton, J.R.Fairman, M.J.Furnell, A.Ll.Lambert, N.Langridge, C.Maggs, R.Randell, E.Staff, N.Stanyon and our ever supportive wives.

GEOGRAPHICAL SETTING

Apart from its southern extremity, the route is situated on the Chalk of the southern flank of Salisbury Plain. South from Andover, the line follows the valley of the River Anton to Fullerton where it joins the line from Longparish, which runs roughly parallel to the upper reaches of the River Test. South to Mottisfont the route is on the eastern side of the Test Valley, on the boundary of the Chalk and Alluvium of the valley floor.

In the Romsey area, Brickheath is traversed but most of the line to Redbridge crosses Gravel. From there to Southampton, the railway was built on or near the foreshore.

The maps at each location in this album are to the scale of 25" to 1 mile.

February 1890

ANDOVER, ROMSEY, and SOUTHAMPTON.—London and South Western.										

[Railway timetable — Down and Up week-day and Sunday services between Waterloo/London and Southampton Docks via Andover, Clatford, Fullerton Junc., Stockbridge, Horsebridge, Mottisfont, Romsey, Nursling, Redbridge, Millbrook, S'hampton.]

HISTORICAL BACKGROUND

The year 1847 was noteworthy in the railway history of the district because passenger services commenced between Salisbury (Milford) and Eastleigh (then Bishopstoke) on 1st March and also between Blechynden (the present Southampton station) and Dorchester on 1st June. Southampton Tunnel opened on 29th July enabling trains to run to London (although they had to reverse at Southampton Terminus until July 1858). These services were operated by the London & South Western Railway who obtained powers in 1847 to build a railway between Andover and Redbridge, but it failed to materialise.

However, LSWR trains arrived at Andover from Basingstoke on 3rd July 1854 and services were extended to Salisbury (Milford) on 1st May 1857.

An independent Andover and Redbridge Railway was promoted in 1858 and after being sought by both the GWR and the LSWR, the latter company gained control and opened it throughout on 6th March 1865, as a single line.

It followed the route of the 1794 canal to Andover and soon acquired the title "Sprat and Winkle".

The remaining development in the area was the opening of a line between Fullerton and Hurstbourne on 1st June 1885. Being of limited value, it was the first to close, passenger services being withdrawn on 6th July 1931. The line north of Longparish was completely closed on 29th May 1934 but the remaining part remained open for freight until 28th May 1956.

Following a steady decline in traffic, passenger services between Andover and Southampton were withdrawn on 7th September 1964. The line was closed completely between Kimbridge Junction (north of Romsey) and Andover Town, where freight facilities remained available until 18th September 1967. The track remained in place for over four years after the passage of the last passenger train.

ANDOVER, ROMSEY, and SOUTHAMPTON.—London and South Western.

July 1914

PASSENGER SERVICES

Initially there were four trains on weekdays, one of which was mixed, and one on Sundays but only three trains on weekdays were shown in the 1869 timetable. By 1890, there were six weekday and two Sunday journeys each way.

The 1906 timetable still showed only two trains on Sundays but eleven on weekdays, three of which ran from northern towns, including Derby and Bradford. One was named the "South Express" and a Saturdays only train was called the "Ocean Boat Express", arriving at Southampton at 8.10am. Through running via the Midland & South Western Junction Railway north of Andover was extended, the "South Express" originating at Manchester (London Road) for a number of years before and after WWI. In the reverse direction the name "Northern Express" was used, these names only being applied north of Andover.

In the summer of 1921, there were nine trains running the full length of the route, two of which were to or from the North. There was no Sunday service, but this was restored in the mid-1920s to a single afternoon journey each way.

A similar service level was maintained until the outbreak of WWII, although the through service was limited to one on weekdays. This was to Liverpool until it was cut back to Cheltenham in the mid-1930s. By 1938 there were also two trips between Andover Junction and Town, together with a morning service between the Town and Horsebridge.

The 1944 timetable showed seven departures south from Andover Junction, with two on Sunday afternoons, only one hour apart. These and both evening weekend trains terminated at Eastleigh. Apart from the addition of one or two weekday trains, little changed until 16th September 1957 when the introduction of DEMUs more than doubled the service, with sixteen weekday and five Sunday trains, all running to Portsmouth via Eastleigh. In June 1962, the Sunday service was doubled, the through train from Cheltenham was withdrawn and the basic hourly service was diverted via Southampton. This timetable was operated until closure of the line north of Romsey in September 1964.

ANDOVER, ROMSEY, and SOUTHAMPTON.—London and South Western.

July 1917

ANDOVER JUNCTION

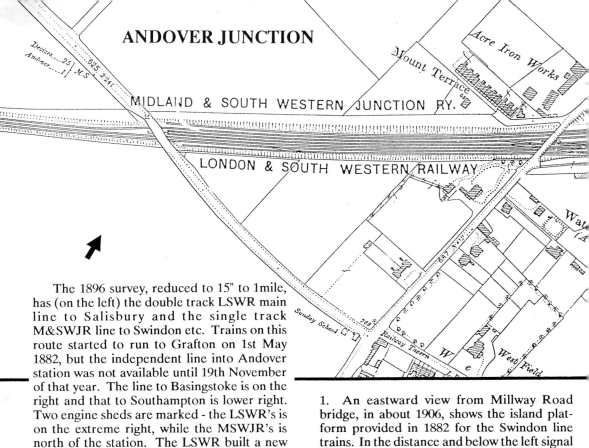

The 1896 survey, reduced to 15" to 1mile, has (on the left) the double track LSWR main line to Salisbury and the single track M&SWJR line to Swindon etc. Trains on this route started to run to Grafton on 1st May 1882, but the independent line into Andover station was not available until 19th November of that year. The line to Basingstoke is on the right and that to Southampton is lower right. Two engine sheds are marked - the LSWR's is on the extreme right, while the MSWJR's is north of the station. The LSWR built a new one in 1904, close to the 50ft. MSWJR turntable. Both sheds remained in use until 1962.

1. An eastward view from Millway Road bridge, in about 1906, shows the island platform provided in 1882 for the Swindon line trains. In the distance and below the left signal arm is the then new LSWR locomotive shed. (Lens of Sutton)

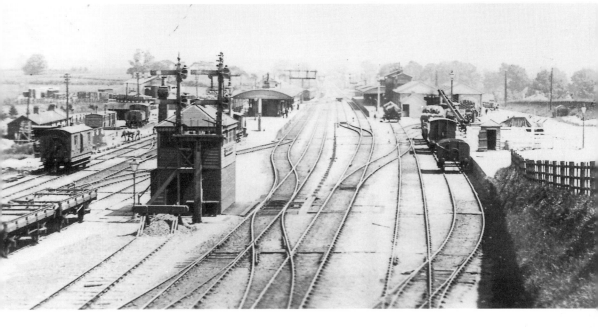

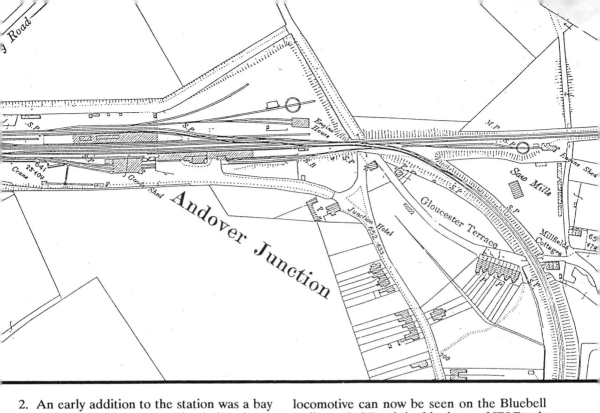

2. An early addition to the station was a bay platform for Southampton trains, built prior to the commencement of services in 1865. Class U no. 31618 waits there with the 11.25am service to Eastleigh on 14th May 1955. This locomotive can now be seen on the Bluebell Railway. "A" Box is in this view and "B" Box is in the previous picture - both opened in 1882 and closed in 1973. (J.H.Aston)

3. Viewed from the bay platform, class T9 no. 30726 arrives with the 8.53am from Portsmouth & Southsea on 26th October 1957. There were no run-round facilities at the bay and so only push-pull units could conveniently terminate there. (D.Cullum)

4. Class M7 no. 30130 is seen close to the signal visible in the background of the previous picture. It is hauling the 12.33pm from Portsmouth & Southsea on 19th October 1957 and is passing over the crossover used by trains departing from the bay. (S.C.Nash)

6. The imposing main building dates from the opening of the line from Basingstoke in 1854 and is seen in 1988 following a major refurbishment carried out in conjunction with the TSB Trust Ltd. Note the new traditional style lamps. The suffix "Junction" was dropped in 1964. (J.Scrace)

5. A view towards London from the island platform in 1957 shows the curved canopy extension serving the down bay platform. The Southampton line diverges beyond the signal box. (D.Cullum)

London & South Western Ry.
This Ticket is issued subject to the Regulations & Conditions stated in the Company's Time Tables & Bills

ANDOVER TOWN to
ANDOVER JUNC.

Andover T.   Andover T.
Andover Junc.   Andover Junc.
3rd CLASS   (S.10) 3rd CLASS
Fare 1d   Fare 1d

7. As part of the 150th anniversary of the opening of the railway to Winchfield, class 4 2-6-4T no. 80080 operated a special train service between Andover and Romsey (via the Laverstock Loop) on 26th September 1988. The shed on the left is part of a fertiliser depot, the sidings for which opened in May 1969. (M.Turvey)

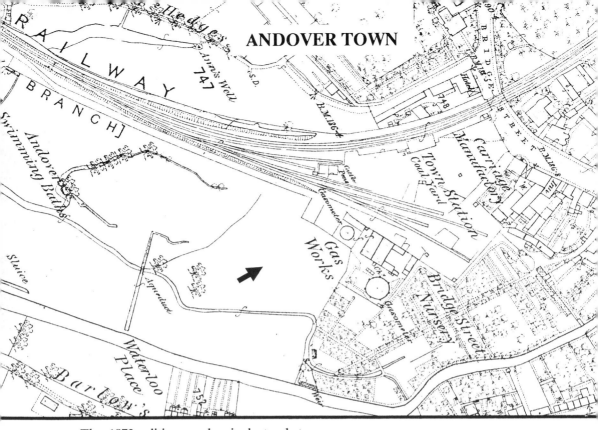

ANDOVER TOWN

The 1873 edition marks single track to Andover Junction on the right. This was doubled in 1882 and the section to Clatford followed in 1884. The gas works had been built adjacent to the Andover & Southampton Canal basin which was infilled to make space for the goods yard.

8. A northward view at the turn of the century shows the wooden footbridge, which was probably erected at the time of the track doubling in 1882. The level crossing over Bridge Street was the cause of public complaint from the outset. (Lens of Sutton)

9. The footbridge was replaced by a SR-built concrete one, with double flights as before. The main building was clad with corrugated iron, a material more commonly seen on the light railways of a later era. (J.H.Aston)

The 1937 map shows little change in the railway facilities, apart from siding lengthening and provision of a goods shed, but the gas works had grown greatly.

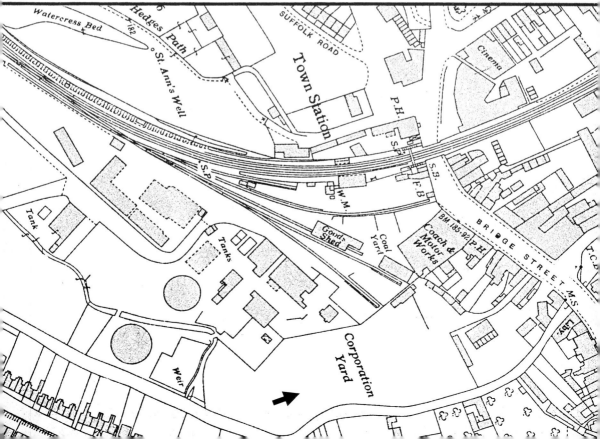

10. This and the previous picture were taken in 1955 when the goods yard was still busy. Adjacent to it were the gas works, electricity works, oil depot, and numerous agricultural stores. (J.H.Aston)

12. The 2.45pm Andover Junction to Southampton Terminus service was propelled by class M7 no. 30109 on 21st November 1959. This train ran via Eastleigh but on Saturdays it terminated at Portsmouth & Southsea at 4.16pm. (S.C.Nash)

←

11. No. 7810 *Draycott Manor* heads the 10.11am from Cheltenham on 14th May 1955. At this period there were two such through trains each day. On the right is the oil store and the massive goods shed. (J.H.Aston)

2nd - SINGLE	SINGLE - 2nd
Andover Town to	
Andover Town Fullerton	Andover Town Fullerton
FULLERTON	
(S) 10d. FARE 10d. (S)	
For condit'ns see over	For condit ns see over

8 0 0 6 5

9600 98

13. The crossover between the platforms is out of view in this 1964 picture. It was so positioned to reduce the duration of closure of the crossing gates which caused massive traffic jams. There was no bypass to the town then and Bridge Street carried all West of England traffic on the A303. (E.Wilmshurst)

14. The capacious goods shed contained a 30cwt crane, one of 7½ ton capacity being available at the Junction. The site is partly occupied by the Trustee Savings Bank's offices and a roundabout from Western Avenue has been built along the trackbed of the line to the former junction. (C.Hall)

15. After the cessation of passenger services on 7th September 1964, the down line was retained for access to the goods yard. The signal box was then used as a ground frame and to control the gates. Most Andover residents were pleased to see its total closure, along with the yard, on 18th September 1967. (C.Hall)

UPPER CLATFORD SIDING

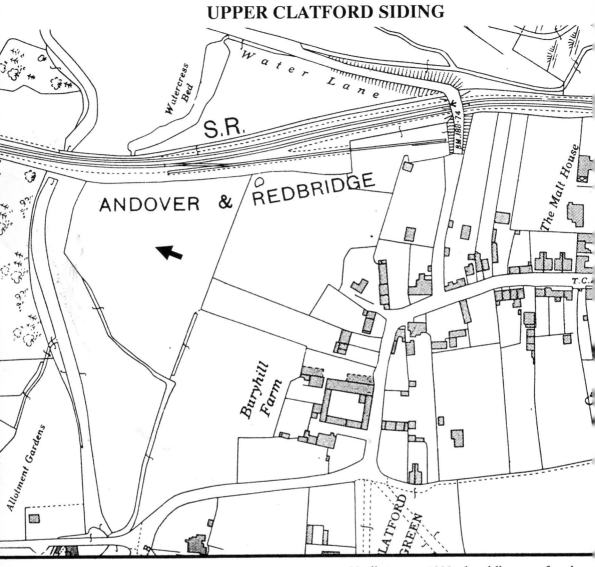

Until August 1933, the siding was for the exclusive use of Taskers, agricultural engineers and traction engine builders of Waterloo Ironworks, one mile to the west. Thereafter and until December 1945 it was available for public use.

16. A northward view from Water Lane Bridge on 4th September 1968 shows the demolition train on the up track, four years after the last scheduled train ran. The siding had earlier diverged from the down line, near the brake van. (J.H.Bird)

CLATFORD

17. Along with the other stations north of Romsey, Clatford opened and closed with the line. This early postcard shows the lack of platform canopies. (Lens of Sutton)

The first edition map of 1872 reveals the arrangement during the single track era. Goodworth Corn Mill was close to the station while Upper Clatford Paper Mill was a short distance upstream, both no doubt generating some rail traffic.

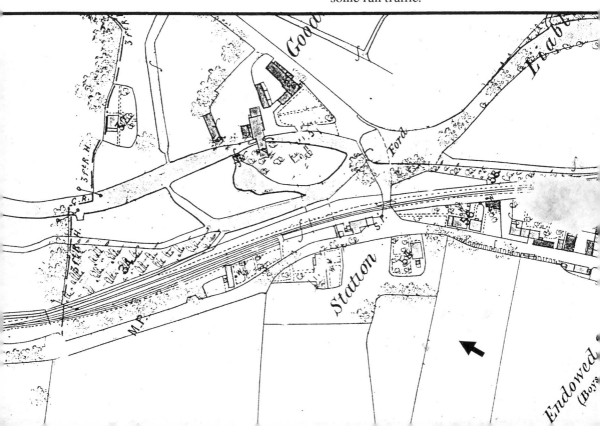

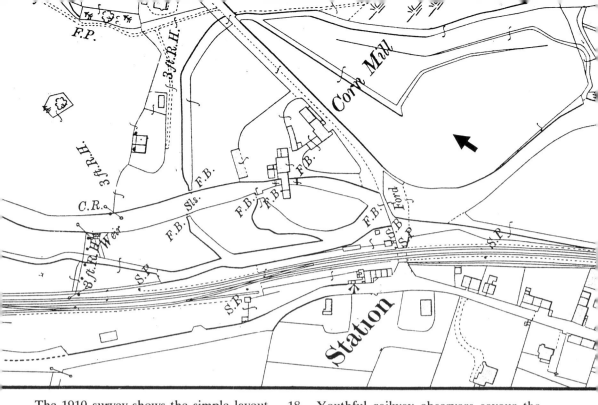

The 1910 survey shows the simple layout which persisted until good services were withdrawn on 3rd October 1960. The proximity of the River Test is evident.

18. Youthful railway observers savour the passage of the 11.40 freight on 17th August 1955. The locomotive is U class 4-6-0 no. 31619 and is seen heading towards Romsey. (J.H.Aston)

19. The ford through the River Anton meant that the lane was little used and on 25th February 1962 the signal box was closed, when crossing was restricted to pedestrians only. The tranquil scene was recorded on 12th October 1957. (J.J.Smith)

20. The station was situated between the small villages of Upper Clatford and Goodworth Clatford. Passengers wait to cross the line as class M7 no. 30379 propels the 5.42pm Andover Junction to Eastleigh on 7th June 1958. (S.C.Nash)

London & South Western Rv.

CLATFORD to

SOUTH'TON WEST

Clatford   Clatford
Soton West   Soton West

THIRD **(S.1)** **THIRD**
CLASS See over **CLASS**

Fare 1/11   Fare 1/11

AP.11.98   4478

21. The station had lost its signal box and siding, but full toilet facilities fortunately remained when photographed in February 1964. (See the cover for another view of Clatford.) (E.Wilmshurst)

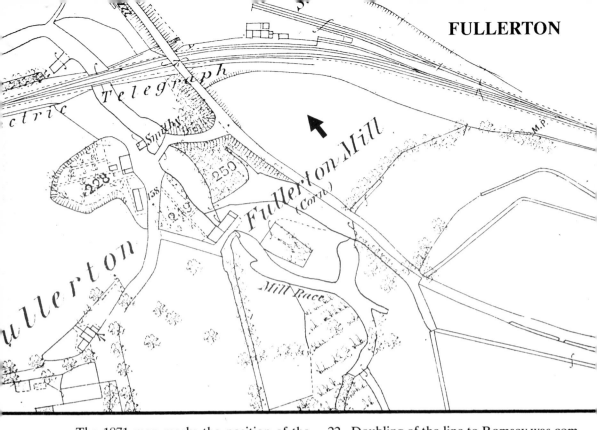

FULLERTON

The 1871 map marks the position of the original station, which was known as Fullerton Bridge until October of that year. The line to Romsey is on the right.

22. Doubling of the line to Romsey was completed in time for the opening of the line from Hurstbourne. A train from Andover stands at the up main platform, the branch platforms being on the right in this northward view. (Lens of Sutton)

23. Looking south at the main platforms from the up sidings, we see a train arriving from Romsey. As there was no subway or footbridge, passengers had to use the crossing at the end of the platforms. (Lens of Sutton)

The 1896 survey indicates the position of the second station which was named Fullerton Junction from May 1889 until July 1929. The line to Longparish and Hurstbourne is top left.

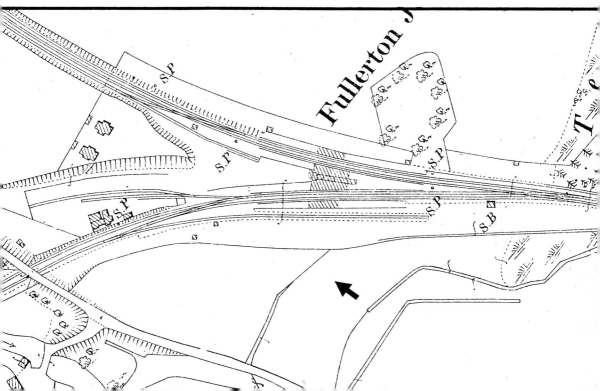

24. The A12 Jubilee class was built between 1887 and 1895 and many were on light duties during the SR period. No. 614 waits with its single coach for the Hurstbourne line, hardly an exhausting task. (Lens of Sutton)

26. A view from the top of the signal featured in the previous picture shows conditions in October 1957. Having closed on 28th May 1956, the Longparish branch was weed covered although part of the track was retained as a siding for the storage of condemned wagons. (D.Cullum)

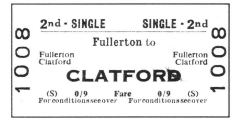

25. A class 700 0-6-0 returns from Longparish on 17th August 1955, having made revenue in the other direction only. There was ten times more traffic onto the branch than from it, in its final years. (J.H.Aston)

27. The up side lost half its roof in about 1956, adding to the air of despair as passengers disappeared. The signal box had 28 levers but only 17 were in use after 1956. (Lens of Sutton)

28. Looking south from the road bridge in 1957, we see part of the original station building on the left. Behind it, and out of view, a siding parallel to the Longparish line was relaid in 1942 for use by the RAF for ammunition traffic. An additional one was provided in 1945. (D.Cullum)

29. The boarded exterior was hungry for paint when photographed in 1957. As late as 1966, the booking office still contained a chalk board to carry information relating to air raids! (S.C.Nash)

30. One of the elegant class T9 "Greyhounds" accelerates north with a train from Portsmouth on 2nd November 1957. The former cattle dock is on the left, its siding remaining usuable until 1964. The siding on the right was taken out of use in December 1957. (S.C.Nash)

31. Ex-LSWR class M7 no. 30028 heads a short train from Eastleigh in the spring of 1958. At this time steam trains were deputising on this route for some of the newly introduced DEMU sets which had been withdrawn temporarily for bogie and coupling modifications. The ground frame on the right controlled the crossover until May 1964. (N.Sprinks)

BRANCH LINE TO LONGPARISH

A line between Fullerton and Hurstbourne was first proposed by the Didcot, Newbury and Southampton Railway as a means of obtaining access to Southampton by joining the LSWR main line at Whitchurch. The line was subsequently built by the LSWR with a view to it serving this purpose, as the Eastleigh area was deemed to be too busy to accommodate additional traffic. In the event, the Whitchurch connection was never completed and DNSR trains did run through Eastleigh.

Thus the double track line from Hurstbourne was a white elephant from its opening on 1st June 1885, serving only sparse local traffic and being of limited value as a diversionary route.

Plans were made in 1906 for a connection at Redbridge to be laid so that Bournemouth and Weymouth trains could run from London via Longparish but the scheme was not fulfilled.

There were five weekday trains in 1887, reduced to four in 1914 and three in 1920. The line was singled throughout on 13th July 1913 and passenger services ceased on 6th July 1931. The Hurstbourne-Longparish section was closed completely on 29th May 1934, the remainder succumbing on 28th May 1956.

32. A northward view of the commencement of the branch in 1957 includes the home and starting signals, which were controlled by levers 9 and 10 respectively. In the distance is the Wherwell Road bridge. (S.C.Nash)

33. An officer's inspection special passes under Wherwell Road on 30th October 1957, seventeen months after the last goods train. During 1957, the branch had been used for testing the new DEMUs prior to their introduction on Hampshire local services. (S.C.Nash)

BASINGSTOKE, WHITCHURCH, and FULLERTON.—L. & S.W.

Waterloo Station,	mrn	mrn	mrn	mrn	mrn	aft	aft
LONDON 48....dep	6 50	9 0	....	1115	1145	....	3 50
Basingstoke......dep	8 27	1016	....	1245	1 32	....	5 21
Oakley	8 37	....	....	1255	1 44	....	5 30
Overton	8 44	....	....	1 2	1 51	....	5 36
Whitchurch 1........	8 58	1035	1115	1 10	1 59	2 40	5 55
Hurstbourne	9 4	⌐	1120	1 15	⌐	2 45	6 0
Long-Parish	9 12	....	1127	1 22	....	2 53	6 7
Wherwell	9 18	....	1132	1 28	....	2 59	6 13
Fullerton Junc. 64.arr	9 22	....	1135	1 31	....	3 3	6 17
64 SOUTHAMPTON DKS.	1021	....	12 32	....	....	4 50	7 24

Docks Station,	mrn	mrn	mrn	aft	aft
64 SOUTHAMPTON ..dep	....	9 45	....	1245	3 5
Fullerton Junc...dep	8 0	1045	1145	1 50	4 20
Wherwell	8 4	1049	1149	1 54	4 32
Long-Parish	8 10	1056	1156	2 0	4 53
Hurstbourne 48......	8 18	11 5	12 5	2 10	5 6
Whitchurch 1	8 33	1181	1210	2 36	5 12
Overton	8 41	1140	1218	2 44	⌐
Oakley	8 49	1148	1225	2 52	....
Basingstoke 49, 8 arr	8 56	1157	1233	3 2	....
LONDON 49......arr	10 5	1 17	2 10	4 43	....

aft
....
....
....
....
....
6 10
6 18
6 25
6 32
7 55

February 1890

July 1906

BASINGSTOKE, WHITCHURCH, and FULLERTON. London and South Western.

Miles	Waterloo Station,	n	n	mrn		n	n			Miles	Town & Dock Station,	n	p	n		mrn	n	n			NOTES.
	120London ....dep	6 40	8 50	1140							126SOUTHAMPTON ..dep			9 15							n Rail Motor Car Service be-
	Basingstoke ......dep	8 18	10 8	1250		1 145	38				Fullerton Junction.dep	7 53	1023			1140	2 55	5 16			tween Whitchurch and
4½	Oakley..............	8 28		1	1	1 25	5 48			1½	Wherwell	7 57	1027			1144	2 29	5 20			Fullerton Junction, 1st and
7½	Overton	8 36		9	2	1 33	5 55			3½	Longparish	8 4	1033			1150	2 36	5 26			3rd class.
11½	Whitchurch †† ... f arr.	8 42	1025	17		1 39	6 1			7½	Hurstbourne 102	8 15	1044			12 12	2 46	5 37			D Leaves Horsebridge at 7 38
	(see above) { dep.	8 59	1055	1		3 56	10			9½	Whitchurch†102 { arr.	8 20	1049			12 62	5 45	42			and Stockbridge at 7 46 mrn.
12½	Hurstbourne........	9 4	11 0	1		3 106	19				and above. { dep.	8 31	1124			12 83		5 55			†† About 1½ miles to Didcot and
17½	Longparish..........	9 13	11 9	1		3 186	24			13	Overton	8 39	1132			1217	3 96	3			Newbury Company's Station.
19½	Wherwell	9 19	1115	1	38	3 246	30			16½	Oakley	122	8 47	1140		1225	3 17	6 12			✠ For other Trains be-
20½	Fullerton Junc. 126.arr	9 22	1118	41		3 286	33			20½	Basingstoke 37, 108, ar	8 54	1150			1235	3 24	6 20			tween Basingstoke & Hurst-
43½	126SOUTHMPTN TN.& DK.	1031	1234	....		5 16	7 45			68½	122London (Waterloo)ar	10 0	1 35			2 35	5 13	7 30			bourne, see pages 102 to107.

WHERWELL

34. Pronounced "Werul", the station was provided with the curved canopies then favoured by the LSWR and used for the extension at Andover Junction. This is the view south - hence the poor lighting.
(Lens of Sutton)

35. The line is on a 40 chain radius through the station with reverse curves of the same dimension at each end - not a recipe for fast running. The signal box had 15 levers and was closed on 13th July 1913. (Lens of Sutton)

WHERWELL STATION.

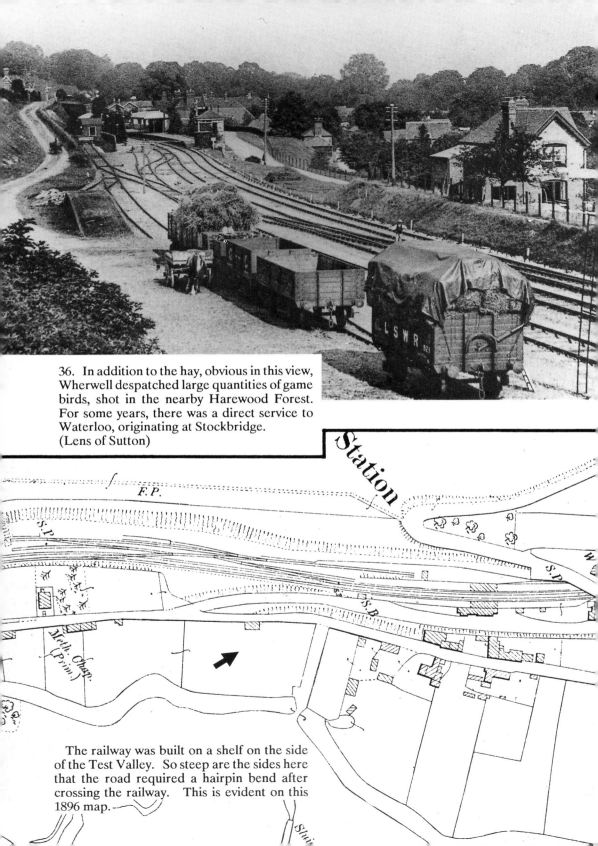

36. In addition to the hay, obvious in this view, Wherwell despatched large quantities of game birds, shot in the nearby Harewood Forest. For some years, there was a direct service to Waterloo, originating at Stockbridge. (Lens of Sutton)

The railway was built on a shelf on the side of the Test Valley. So steep are the sides here that the road required a hairpin bend after crossing the railway. This is evident on this 1896 map.

37. The booking hall had an elaborate railed porch at its entrance, above which a dormer window was fitted. This gave additional illumination to the hall. The eastern gates to the drive can be seen in the distance.
(Lens of Sutton)

38. A wagonless freight service waits for the photographer on 17th August 1955, by which time there was only one siding at Wherwell and the branch expenses were twice that of income.
(J.H.Aston)

BASINGSTOKE, WHITCHURCH, and FULLERTON.—London and South Western.										
Miles	**Week Days only.**				Miles		**Week Days only.**			
	Waterloo Station,	mrn	mrn	aft	aft		157 Southampton Towndep	mrn	mrn	aft	aft
	160 London ....dep	6 35	11 40	2 10	3 50		Fullerton Junction....dep	p 9 45	12 45	3 43
—	Basingstoke ....dep	8 14	....	3 19	5 07	—	Wherwell	....	7 47	11 32	2 55 21
4¼	Oakley	8 25	....	3 29	5 48	1¼	Longparish	....	7 54	11 38	2 35 5 31
7¾	Overton................	8 32	....	3 37	5 55	3½	Hurstbourne 128	....	8 6	11 49	2 46 5 42
11¼	Whitchurch † 42 ... {arr.	8 39	....	3 43	6 1	7½	Whitchurch † 42, {arr.	....	8 10	11 54	2 51 5 47
	{dep.	8 59	....	3 73	5 36 6 10	9¼	128 {dep.	....	8 26	11 56	3 06 6 5
13¾	Hurstbourne	9 4	....	3 22	5 56 6 15	13	Overton	....	8 33	12 43	7 6 13
17¾	Longparish	9 13	....	4 14	7 6 24	16½	Oakley ......(156, 162)	....	8 41	12 13	156 21
19¼	Wherwell	9 19	....	4 6 4	5 6 59	20¼	Basingstoke 31, 134.. arr.	....	8 51	12 23	2 56 6 2
20¾	Fullerton Junction 157 ar.	9 21	....	4 9 4	15 6 92	68½	162 London (Waterloo)arr.	....	10 11	3 15	17 8 10
43	157 Southampton Town§arr.	10 27	....	5 23	7 55					

h Via Eastleigh.   D Leaves Stockbridge at 7 35 mrn., see page 157.   r Southampton West.
† One mile to Didcot and Newbury Company's Station.   § Station for Docks.
☞ For **OTHER TRAINS** between Basingstoke and Hurstbourne, see page 123.

39. The first of three 1957 photographs shows the inclination of the road bridge and the severity of the reverse curves. Chalk falls were a problem in all the cuttings, particularly the deeper ones near Hurstbourne. (S.C.Nash)

BASINGSTOKE, WHITCHURCH, and FULLERTON.—London and South Western.									
Miles	**Week Days only.**				Miles		**Week Days only.**		
	Waterloo Station,	mrn	aft	aft		Southampton Towndep	mrn	mrn	mrn	aft
	128 London ....dep	6 25	2 10	3 50			p	....	7 20	....	3 43
—	Basingstoke ....dep	8 15	3 30	5 41	—	Fullerton Junc.(above)dep	7 42	....	9 40	....	5 25
4¼	Oakley	8 26	3 41	5 52	1¼	Wherwell	7 47	....	9 44	....	5 28
7¾	Overton................	8 34	3 48	5 59	3½	Longparish	7 54	....	9 50	....	5 55
11¼	Whitchurch † 42 ... {arr.	8 42	3 55	6 6	7½	Hurstbourne 140	8 6	....	10 11	....	5 46
	{dep.	8 52	4 1	6 14	9¼	Whitchurch † 42, {arr.	8 10	....	10 6	....	5 51
13¾	Hurstbourne	8 55	4 6	6 19		140 {dep.	8 24	....	10 32	11 27	6 19
17¾	Longparish	9 4	4 15	6 28	13	Overton .... arr.	8 32	....	....	11 35	6 29
19¼	Wherwell	9 10	4 21	6 34	16½	Oakley .....(134, 148)	8 40	....	....	1144	6 37
20¾	Fullerton Junc.(above)arr.	9 12	4 25	6 36	20¼	Basingstoke 46, 123, "	8 49	....	10 56	11 59	6 46
43	Southampton Town§arr.	10 27	5 31	10 43	68½	134 London (Waterloo)arr.	10 11	....	11 54	....	8 27

h Via Eastleigh.   D Leaves Stockbridge at 7 35 mrn., see above.
† About 1¼ miles to Didcot and Newbury Company's Station.   § Station for Docks.
☞ For **LOCAL TRAINS** between Basingstoke and Hurstbourne, see page 140.

40. A standard station plan was used and so stations of similar design can be found at widespread locations, ranging from Wareham to Worplesdon and Swanwick to Swaythling. (J.J.Smith)

41. The site was sold to Andover Rural District Council for development. The building was retained for residential purposes and bungalows were built each side of it. Back in 1927, the line had been used for the filming of a silent version of "The Ghost Train". (J.J.Smith)

LONGPARISH

42. No. 614, seen earlier at Fullerton, waits with one passenger in evidence, probably on the last day of public services. The second track was replaced in 1942 to form a station loop for wartime use. (Lens of Sutton)

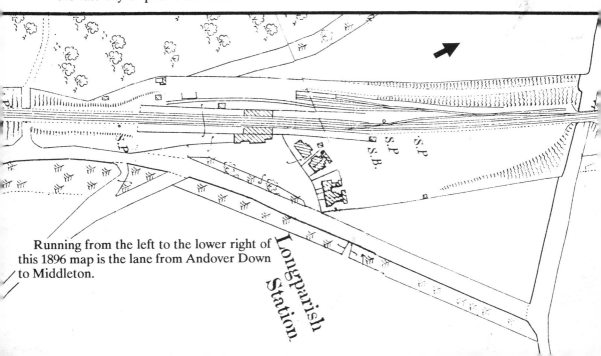

Running from the left to the lower right of this 1896 map is the lane from Andover Down to Middleton.

Longparish Station.

43. The station was 1½ miles from Longparish, an attractive village situated close to the River Test. The stone above the front door of the house reads "AD1884". (J.H.Aston)

44. Until 1942, the sidings faced north. At this time they were relaid in the opposite direction and extended to serve extensive RAF ammunition stores. This and the next two photographs were taken on 17th August 1955. (J.H.Aston)

45. The hard standing between the tracks had been in use by the RAF until January 1955, it having taken ten years to dispose of the explosives. This was the sole reason for the line remaining open for so long. (J.H.Aston)

46. The train crew, a clerk and an inspector pose amidst rural tranquility. In 1954 the branch forwarded 189 tons of goods and received 350 tons along with 1350 tons of fuel. Back in the 1920s, Taylor's Sawmills had required up to 30 wagons per day. (J.H.Aston)

47.   An overhead crane had been installed during WWII and up to 15 mobile cranes were in use handling bombs of all sizes up to 4000lbs. In April 1944, four trains a day were running and nearly 1200 wagons were loaded and unloaded.   After the war, transit camps were established, as many as 14 troop trains being handled in a day.   (Lens of Sutton)

48.   This sign was displayed on the corner of the booking office in June 1958, over two years after freight services ceased.   In 1954, the branch was staffed by one clerk, who served both stations and received £402 per annum. (S.C.Nash)

WHITCHURCH and FULLERTON.—Southern.									
Miles		**Week Days only.**			Miles		**Week Days only.**		
		mrn	aft	a			b	mrn	aft
—	145 London (Waterloo) dep.	6 30	3 30	5 0	—	Fullerton Junction......dep.	7 29	10 10	6 10
—	Whitchurch..........dep.	9 5	5 13	6 50	1¼	Wherwell	7 33	10 13	6 13
1¼	Hurstbourne	9 10	5 18	6 55	3¼	Longparish	7 40	10 20	6 20
6	Longparish	9 21	5 27	7 4	7¼	Hurstbourne	7 52	10 31	6 31
8	Wherwell ....[174	9 26	5 32	7 9	9¼	Whitchurch** ,145 arr.	7 57	10 36	6 36
9¼	Fullerton Junc. 170, arr.	9 30	5 36	7 13	68¼	152 London (Waterloo) arr.	9 57	12 16	8 20

a Through Train to Southampton Terminus, see page 172.   b Runs from Southampton Terminus, see page 174.
** About 1¼ miles to G. W. (late D. N. & S.) Station.

July 1924

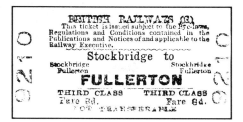

49. The fourth vehicle is passing over the River Test as 4300 class no. 6341 runs over the crossover by Fullerton down home signal on 26th October 1957. The train is the 10.15am from Cheltenham Spa (Lansdown) to Southampton Terminus. The 2.0pm departure from Cheltenham was generally hauled by a Southern Region class U1. (J.J.Smith)

50. The chalk from cuttings and hillsides was used to infill the canal prior to railway building. A train of four-wheelers runs north behind no. 427, a class 415, built in 1883 and withdrawn in 1921. (D.Cullum coll.)

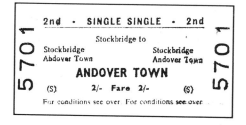

51. A class M7 propels its train past the clear fishing waters of the Test, in the Spring of 1958, during the belated swansong of steam on the line. A neat garden surrounds the PW hut, a long lost custom. (N.Sprinks)

52. The 10.15am from Cheltenham is seen near Leckford early in 1958, this service being withdrawn that summer. The locomotive is no. 7808 *Cookham Manor*, now cared for by the Great Western Society at Didcot. (N.Sprinks)

STOCKBRIDGE

53. The station was situated at the east end of the wide main street of this charming small town of under 700 inhabitants. A down train passes under the wooden footbridge, which was retained until the end. Note the large signal sighting board. (Lens of Sutton)

54. Four photographs taken on 26th October 1957 show all aspects of the station. This is the view north from the footbridge, featuring the then new agricultural merchant's store on the right. (D.Cullum)

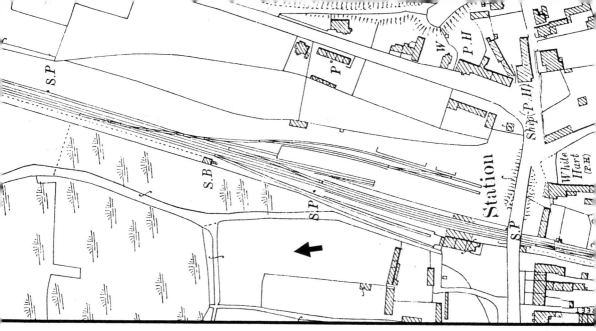

The 1896 edition shows the goods yard at its optimum. The 1871 map indicated a similar layout but with a wagon turntable in the easternmost siding.

55. Class M7 no. 30033 restarts the 11.44am Portsmouth & Southsea to Andover Junction on 26th October 1957. The dock on the left has a cattle pen just visible above the buffer stops. The siding was used for race horse traffic to and from local stables prior to 1910. (D.Cullum)

56. The main slate hung buildings faced the town and were much more imposing than the "tin" affair offered to the residents of Andover, a town many times larger. Double entrance doors and an extended urinal were provided for the crowds on race days (D.Cullum)

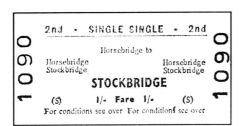

| 2nd · SINGLE SINGLE · 2nd |
| Horsebridge to |
| Horsebridge   Horsebridge |
| Stockbridge   Stockbridge |
| **STOCKBRIDGE** |
| (S)   1/- Fare 1/-   (S) |
| For conditions see over For conditions see over |

57. The 10.15am from Cheltenham called at all stataions between Andover and Romsey, except Clatford. No. 6341 retards its lengthy train as it passes the goods yard, which closed on 21st January 1963. The local trout fishing had once brought "a good class of passenger". (D. Cullum)

ATALANTA, NO. 167, A BEATTIE'S PATENT LOCOMOTIVE, BUILT
AT NINE ELMS WORKS IN 1859 AND USED ON THE ANDOVER
AND REDBRIDGE RAILWAY.

58. Speed record breaking *City of Truro* passed through in 1958, having been in York Museum until 1956. The crossover at the south end of the station was not worked directly from the signal box, there being a ground frame nearby. (N.Sprinks)

59. The throbbing of DEMUs became a familiar sound for the last seven years of the life of the northern part of the route. Unit no. 1105 was strengthened to three cars after being photographed in 1958, bound for Andover Junction. (N.Sprinks)

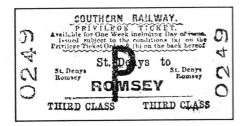

SOUTHERN RAILWAY.
PRIVILEGE TICKET.
Available for One Week including Day of issue.
Issued subject to the conditions (a) on the
Privilege Ticket Order (b) on the back hereof
St. Denys to
St. Denys   St. Denys
Romsey   Romsey
ROMSEY
THIRD CLASS   THIRD CLASS
0249   0249

60. No. D6516 propels the demolition train north on 4th September 1968, having passed under the A30 roadbridge, which was levelled soon after. A roundabout was constructed later, using a corner of the former goods yard. (J.H.Bird)

HORSEBRIDGE

61. The River Test flows through three channels in this part of the valley, the easternmost one passing under the railway north of the station. The tiny village is to the east and the larger community of King's Somborne is one mile further east. (Lens of Sutton)

The 1908 edition shows that the mill race
passes under the northern crossover.

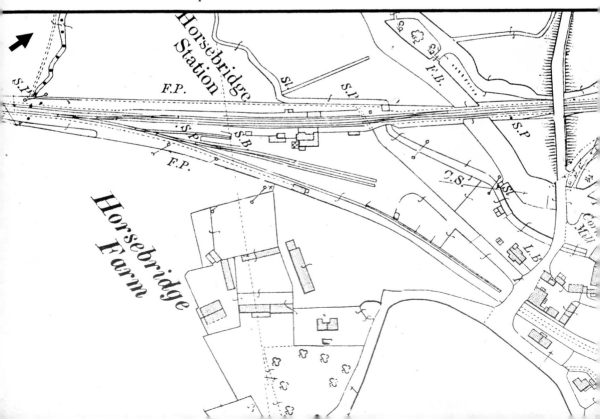

62.   A classical staff group pose on the up platform, complete with a named barrow. The youngest porter would be expected to use this to make deliveries within the village. (Lens of Sutton)

63.   Barrels and a dog add to the diversity of traffic. Also observe that gentlemen using the toilet had the luxury of a roof, albeit well spaced from the wall. The house is now in use as a dwelling. (Lens of Sutton)

64. The small goods shed was on the platform (left), merchandise being handled for Houghton and Broughton, substantial villages on the other side of the valley with direct road access to the station. (J.H.Aston)

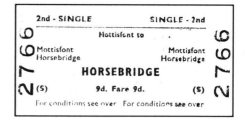

65. This and the previous picture were taken on 17th August 1955. The 4.12pm from Andover Junction is hauled by class 2 2-6-2T no. 41304 and is composed of post-war steel panelled corridor coaches of Bulleid's design. (J.H.Aston)

66. On 5th September 1964, the last day of scheduled services, the "Anton and Test Valley Railtour" was operated from Winchester Chesil to Ludgershall, returning to Eastleigh. Goods services had been withdrawn on 31st December 1962. (J.H.Bird)

MOTTISFONT

67. The slotted signal post was one of the last survivors of its type in the South of England and would earlier have had arms within the slot. When photographed in July 1953, it carried the up distant externally. The finial was also wooden. (D.Cullum)

68. The down platform appears to have suffered from settlement as the morning service from Cheltenham waits to leave behind 4300 class no. 7321 on 17th August 1955. This remnant of the prestigious "South Express" had, by then, poor connections from the Midlands and North, which no doubt contributed to its demise. (J.H.Aston)

The 1897 survey shows the single siding and marks the bed of the Andover Canal filled with reeds. There was no siding in the single line era.

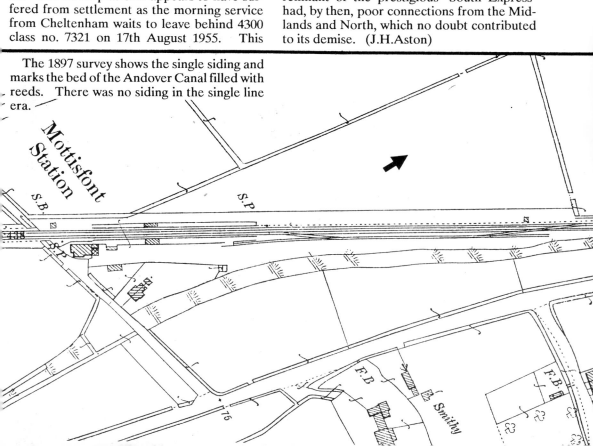

Mottisfont Station

S.B.

138

S.P

S.P

N

F.B

F.B

Smithy

76

69. On 5th October 1957, the 1.42pm Andover Junction to Portsmouth & Southsea was headed by class T9 no. 30288, coupled to an eight-wheeled tender. The small goods yard was closed on 3rd October 1960. (S.C.Nash)

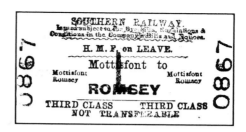

SOUTHERN RAILWAY.
Issued subject to the Bye-laws, Regulations &
Conditions in the Company's Bills and Notices.

H. M. F. on LEAVE.

Mottisfont to
Mottisfont
Romsey

ROMSEY

Mottisfont
Romsey

THIRD CLASS   THIRD CLASS
NOT TRANSFERABLE

70. The up platform predates the down one and was also subject to settlement. The northward extension was constructed with the concrete "harps and slabs", favoured by the SR. The population of the village was little over 500. (C.L.Caddy)

71. The wheel in the box was no longer functional when no. D6525 rumbled past in August 1969, having positioned wagons for the dismantling gang. The house and one gate post were still to be seen in 1990, on the lane east from the village. The present Mottisfont station is on the Salisbury line, south of the village of about 400 residents. (J.H.Bird)

KIMBRIDGE JUNCTION

72. The Andover line is on the right and that to Salisbury on the left. This and the next picture were taken on 12th April 1967 - hence the lack of signal arms on the branch. A ground frame was installed for the demolition trains. (D.Cullum)

73. The signal box was opened on 21st March 1943 in connection with new goods loops to the south. The box closed on 14th June 1967, its predecessor having been on the other side of the track.. Automatic half barriers were brought into use on that date. (D.Cullum)

74. Kimbridge is in the background, as the 10.55am Bristol Temple Meads to Portsmouth Harbour races past Awbridge sidings on 5th October 1957. The four goods loops were laid in 1943 to ease congestion for wartime traffic. (S.C.Nash)

75. Class M7 no. 30130 runs north with an Andover Junction service on 5th October 1957. The outer loops had been taken out of service on 21st June 1948 and the remaining pair followed on 8th June 1952, having been used to store condemned locomotives in 1948-49. (S..C.Nash)

ROMSEY

76. The station opened to passengers on 9th March 1847, being an intermediate one on the Bishopstoke (now Eastleigh) - Salisbury (Milford) branch. Goods services had started on 27th January. This photograph shows the square windowed extension to the building which had been built at a later date (R.C.Riley)

77. With the opening of the Andover- Southampton route in 1865, the station became a junction for four routes but was never described as such. The short platform canopies were extended, as seen, in 1884. (Lens of Sutton)

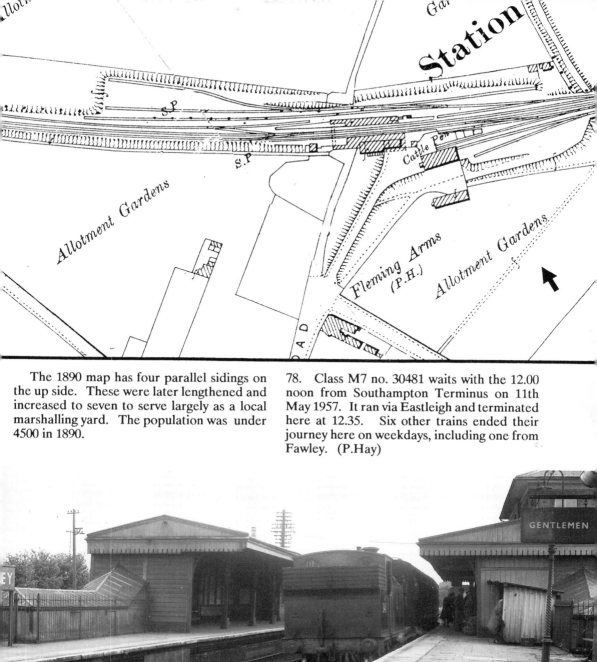

The 1890 map has four parallel sidings on the up side. These were later lengthened and increased to seven to serve largely as a local marshalling yard. The population was under 4500 in 1890.

78. Class M7 no. 30481 waits with the 12.00 noon from Southampton Terminus on 11th May 1957. It ran via Eastleigh and terminated here at 12.35. Six other trains ended their journey here on weekdays, including one from Fawley. (P.Hay)

79.   An eastward view features the massive water tank above the gentleman's toilet, the former still supplying the latter in 1990. When photographed in 1964, the tank was still connected to the locomotive supply columns. Note the alteration in subway protection, when compared with the previous picture.   By then the population was around 6500.
(C.L.Caddy)

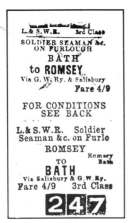

80. No. 34057 *Biggin Hill* is signalled for the
Eastleigh line on 9th April 1967. The tour
from London ran via Salisbury, Fawley, Lym-
ington Pier, Basingstoke, Reading and Alder-
shot. Steam traction was abolished three
months later. (J.H.Bird)

81.   Having terminated at the down platform, DEMU no. 1126 uses the crossover prior to returning to Eastleigh on 4th May 1969, the last day of operation of regular services on this line. In 1990, a single track remained open for freight traffic and diverted passenger services. (J.H.Bird)

83.   A 1988 view includes the roofed water
tank, half way along the down platform and a
3-aspect signal, with route indicator, at its east
end. This was erected in 1979 to facilitate the
reversal of local trains. (J.Scrace)

84. Most of the principal LSWR stations built
in the 1840s had fenestrated or coupled
chimneys and Romsey's is a rare survivor. The
station had a major face lift and is seen re-
freshed in March 1988. (J.Scrace)

82.   Colour light signals are in position, the
installation being completed in 1976.   The
goods yard was closed on 20th July 1970, but
several sidings were retained for use by the
engineers, one still remaining 20 years later.
(Lens of Sutton)

85.   On the left, a bridge with only 8ft. 6ins. headroom accommodates a road to industrial premises.   The soil pipe marks the boundary of the extension to the house - the booking office is at the middle floor level.   (V.Mitchell)

87.   A train from Eastleigh was the vantage point for this photograph of the box at the junction in May 1969.   It was probably built in 1865 and remained in use until 17th October 1982, the timber portion being subsequently craned onto a new base at Romsey Infants School.   Bulk urea wagons stand in the dock siding.   (J.H.Bird)

86.   The goods shed was still standing in 1990 and was unusual in having two levels and a weighbridge still in place at its west end.   The goods yard once had a 7½ ton capacity crane. (C.Hall)

Other views of Kimbridge Junction and Romsey can be found in the companion album *Fareham to Salisbury.*

88. No. 56062 heads an empty stone train from Ardingly to Whatley Quarry on 13th April 1988 and is leaving the Eastleigh line. The Southampton route curves to the right to pass the site of Wills siding, which was on the up side between 1928 and 1959, being mainly used for coal for a nearby nursery. (J.Scrace)

NURSLING

89.   The station opened on 19th November 1883 and was of similar design to those seen at Wherwell and Longparish.   The motive is difficult to understand as the population of the area was best measured in dozens. (Lens of Sutton)

This 1910 map marks the siding to the LSWR's gravel pit. The line is shown on the 1896 edition but had gone by 1918. Ten years later, pits were opened up, further south, to provide gravel for use in constructing the new Test Bridge. Contractors laid down a single track parellel to and east of the main line. Their 0-6-0ST *Seafield No. 4* (Hudswell Clarke no. 1061 of 1914) was still to be seen in its shed in 1937.

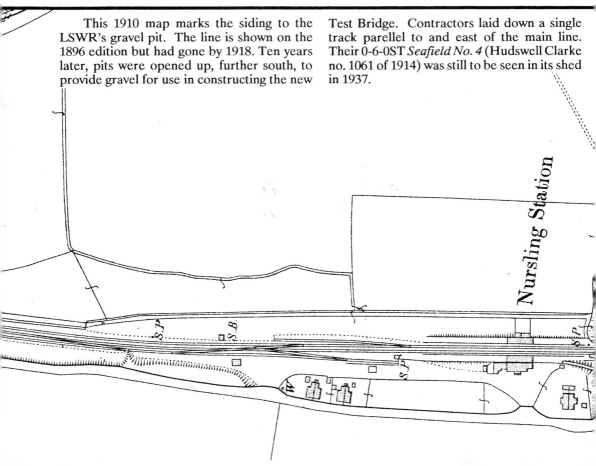

Nursling Station

90. The up siding (right of centre) was taken out of use in 1932 and the signal box was closed on 25th March 1965, following vandalism. Part of the down platform is boarded to facilitate the handling of milk churns. (Lens of Sutton)

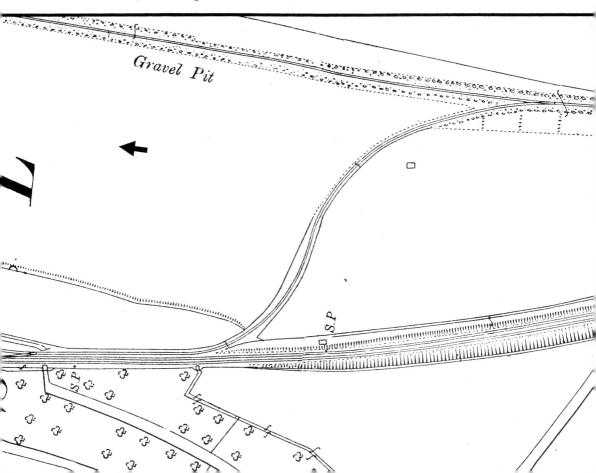

Gravel Pit

S.P.

S.P.

91.   Class 4 2-6-0 no. 76019 arrives with a Portsmouth & Southsea service on 22nd May 1957. The station was completely closed later that year, on 16th September. (H.C.Casserley)

0381
SOUTHERN RAILWAY.
Hants County
Mental Hospital
VISITOR
Available on Day of issue Only
Knowle Platform to
ROMSEY
Third Class
FOR CONDITIONS
SEE BACK
SOUTHERN RAILWAY
Hants County
Mental Hospital
VISITOR
Available on Day of issue Only
Romsey   to
KNOWLE PLATFORM
Third   Class
0381

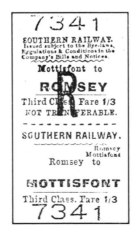

7341
SOUTHERN RAILWAY.
Issued subject to the Bye-laws,
Regulations & Conditions in the
Company's Bills and Notices.
Mottisfont to
ROMSEY
Third Class Fare 1/3
NOT TRANSFERABLE.
- - - - - - - - - - - - - -
SOUTHERN RAILWAY.
Romsey
Mottisfont
Romsey to
MOTTISFONT
Third Class. Fare 1/3
7341

0214
SOUTHERN RAILWAY.
Commercial Traveller
Available on Day of issue only
WIMBORNE to
MILLBROOK
Third Class
FOR CONDITIONS
SEE BACK
SOUTHERN RAILWAY.
Day Commercial
Traveller
Available on Day of issue only
Millbrook to
WIMBORNE
Third   Class
0214

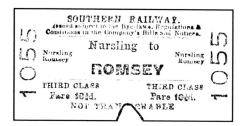

92.   Behind no. 33022 is the former station house; the offices have long gone. The train is the 06.45 Cardiff Central to Portsmouth Harbour on 6th June 1983. Travellers wishing to locate this site should note that it is close to the third overbridge north of Redbridge. (C.Hall)

93. Until 18th November 1930, all road traffic westwards from Southampton used a narrow stone bridge over the River Test, the approach to which is on the left. No. 33040 is on the site of the associated level crossing which was controlled by Test Gates signal box until that day. The train is the 12.06 from Cardiff Central on 26th April 1988. (J.S.Petley)

95. No. 33018 has just passed under the widened A35 bridge and over the junction with the Bournemouth line, as it approaches Redbridge station on 18th May 1985. (M.Turvey)

94. Viewed from the latest road bridge on 14th May 1988, nos. 33112 and 33026 head a railtour from Waterloo to South Wales. It was the "Crompton Farewell" which marked the end of class 33 haulage on passenger services in the South. In the background is part of Redbridge Works. (J.H.Bird)

London & South Western Ry.
This Ticket is issued subject to the Regulations & Conditions stated in the Company's Time Tables & Bills

ROMSEY to
FULLERTON JUNC.
Romsey   Romsey
Fullerton Junc.   Fullerton Junc.
3rd CLASS (S.2)   3rd CLASS
Fare 1/0½   Fare 1/0½

96. Passing over the same crossing to the works that we saw in the previous picture, class T9 no. 30284 shunts an assortment of timber and tankers nearly 30 years earlier, on 22nd May 1957. On the left, the Redbridge Works shunter stands in its shed. (H.C.Casserley)

97. The works shunter that day was a class C14, one of the ten built in 1906-07 as 2-2-0Ts to work on light passenger duties. Originally numbered 745, this engine was rebuilt as an 0-4-0T in 1913. (H.C.Casserley)

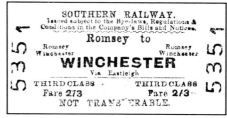

98. The signal box remained in use until 28th February 1982 and is seen on 25th March 1967, along with a cage containing gas cylinders for point heating in frosty weather. (J.Scrace)

REDBRIDGE

99. The station opened with a line to Dorchester on 1st June 1847, only single track being laid initially. An Edwardian view west shows its modest proportions and the junction signals, the distant being for Test Gates level crossing. (Lens of Sutton)

→

100. Looking in the other direction about eighty years later, it is clear that the station had changed little, apart from platform lengthening. Redbridge Works is on the right and the

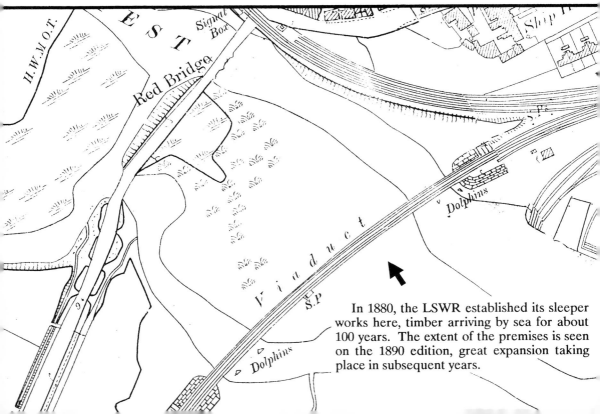

In 1880, the LSWR established its sleeper works here, timber arriving by sea for about 100 years. The extent of the premises is seen on the 1890 edition, great expansion taking place in subsequent years.

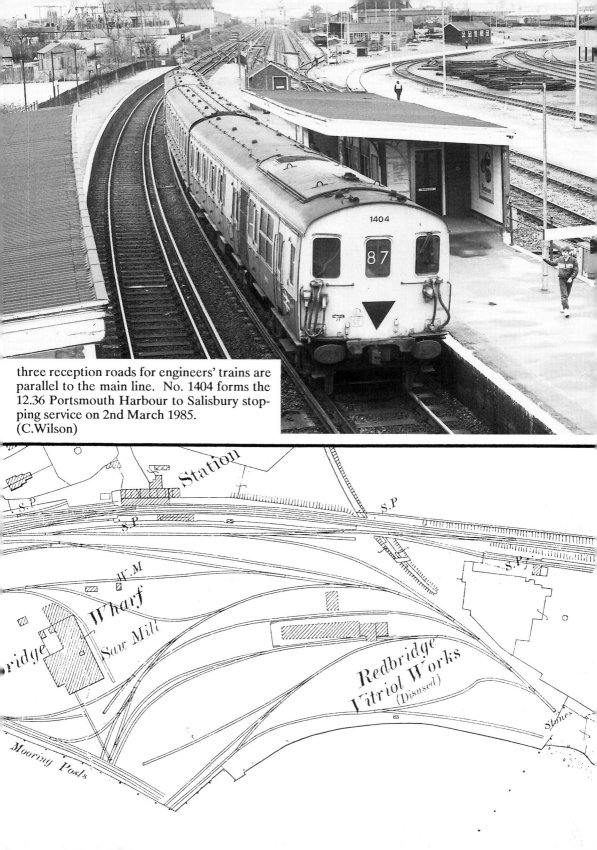

three reception roads for engineers' trains are parallel to the main line. No. 1404 forms the 12.36 Portsmouth Harbour to Salisbury stopping service on 2nd March 1985.
(C.Wilson)

101. Three photographs from 21st August 1985 show Redbridge Works in decline. Very little timber was used by then, its main function being the production of point components and castings, along with the butt welding of conductor rails. The locomotive is no. 09025 and the station footbridge is in the background. (V.Mitchell)

102. At the west end of the foundry, over 50 tons of assorted track components were stacked each week. A steady run-down brought closure of the entire works in 1989, work being undertaken by outside contractors subsequently. (V.Mitchell)

103. The raw materials for the foundry passed through this entrance. This consisted mainly of scrapped chairs, the flux being limestone. The extended dust separators were a late addition. (V.Mitchell)

MILLBROOK

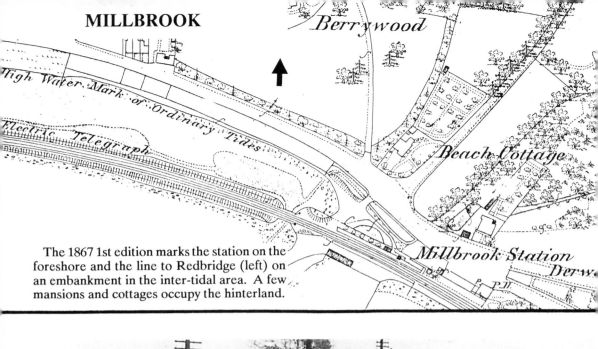

The 1867 1st edition marks the station on the foreshore and the line to Redbridge (left) on an embankment in the inter-tidal area. A few mansions and cottages occupy the hinterland.

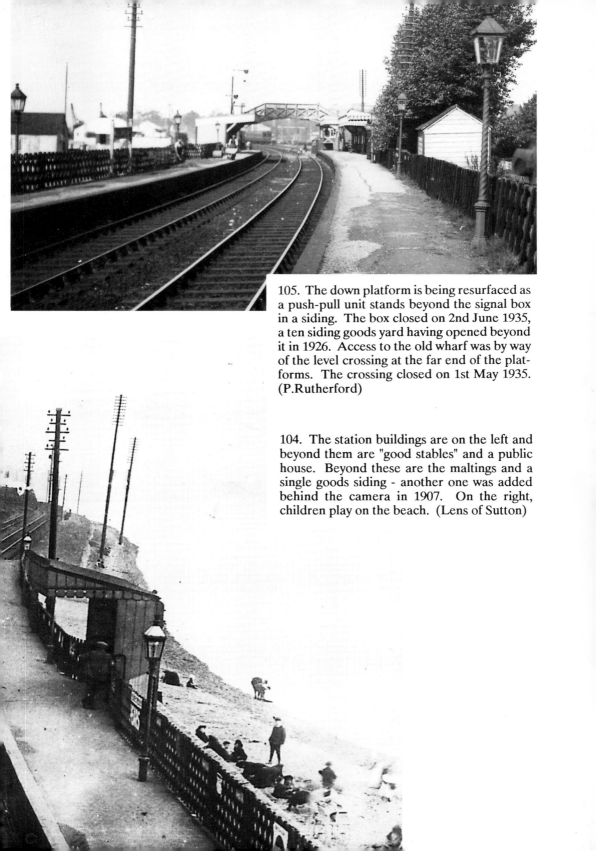

105. The down platform is being resurfaced as a push-pull unit stands beyond the signal box in a siding. The box closed on 2nd June 1935, a ten siding goods yard having opened beyond it in 1926. Access to the old wharf was by way of the level crossing at the far end of the platforms. The crossing closed on 1st May 1935. (P.Rutherford)

104. The station buildings are on the left and beyond them are "good stables" and a public house. Beyond these are the maltings and a single goods siding - another one was added behind the camera in 1907. On the right, children play on the beach. (Lens of Sutton)

106. The old down platform was rebuilt and extended to form an island platform, prior to opening of quadruple track to Southampton Central on 2nd June 1935. This 1966 view of the west end shows the unusual collection of banner repeater signals and insulators ready to receive conductor rails for the Bournemouth electrification, which commenced on 10th July 1967. (D.Fereday Glenn)

107. Class 2 no. 41299 blows off on the south side of the goods shed on 21st April 1966. The yard closed on 31st July 1967 and was relaid to become Millbrook Freightliner Terminal on 7th January 1968. (D.Fereday Glenn)

108. No. 47646 with the 11.10 Portsmouth Harbour to Cardiff has left the quadruple track on 2nd February 1988 and is passing the west end of the Freightliner Terminal. The lines on the right lead to the Maritime Freight Terminal, an additional terminal opened on 28th February 1972 to meet the vast increase in container traffic. (M.Turvey)

109. An eastward view from the footbridge shows part of the extensive area of land (400 acres) reclaimed from the Test in the early 1930s by the SR to form the Western Docks. The two up tracks are on the left, while the two tracks on the extreme right lead into the Western Docks. Acres of Renaults await distribution. (Lens of Sutton)

110. Looking east from the same footbridge on 5th April 1980, we see no. 33106 with the 11.40 Poole to Newcastle passing the Freightliner Terminal. Stopping trains use the tracks each

side of the signal box, which closed on 8th
November 1981 when semaphore signalling
was abolished. (J.Scrace)

ANDOVER, ROMSEY, and SOUTHAMPTON.—London and South Western.

		Week Days.	Suns.
Mls.	Waterloo Station, 102 London ...... dep.		
—	Andover Junction ... dep.		
	" Town		
2¼	Clatford		
5¼	Fullerton Junction 97.		
8¼	Stockbridge		
11¼	Horsebridge		
14	Mottisfont		
18	Romsey 102, 105		
22	Nursling		
23¾	Redbridge 108		
25	Millbrook		
26¾	Southampton West		
28	" (Town & Dock) arr.		

			Week Days.	Suns.
Mls	Town & Dock Station, Southampton ...... dep.			
—	Southampton West.			
1¼	Millbrook			
4¼	Redbridge			
6	Nursling			
10	Romsey 102, 105			
14	Mottisfont			
16¾	Horsebridge			
19¾	Stockbridge			
22¾	Fullerton Junction 97.			
25¾	Clatford			
27¾	Andover Town ... [105]			
28	" Jnc. 101, 102, arr.			
94½	105 Londn (Waterloo) arr.			

July 1906

111. Known as Blechynden until July 1858, the first station was a modest single storey structure to the east of this, its successor. Completed in 1895, it is seen from the north-east, the direction from which the majority of passengers would arrive. (Lens of Sutton)

112. This is another view of the second station, with luggage being loaded into the van at the rear of an up train. The platforms were built on brick arches, which are still visible today. (Lens of Sutton)

113. A view from the south-east includes two pairs of iron gates, two men up a telegraph pole and Blechynden Street level crossing. This closed on 25th June 1934 and the signal box followed on 2nd June 1935. (Lens of Sutton)

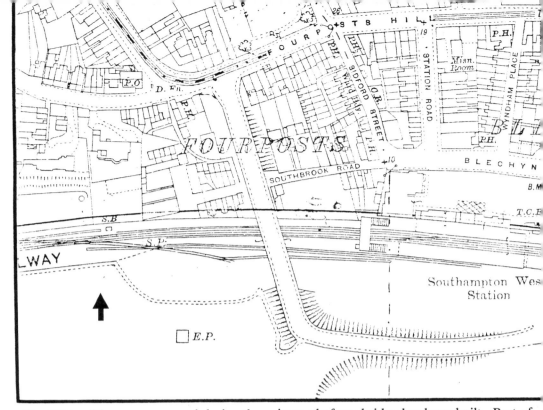

The 1934 edition was prepared during the rebuilding of the station when two extra through platforms were added. The public footbridge at the end of Blechynden Street has been lengthened but only half of the new inter-platform bridge has been built. Part of the first station had earlier been incorporated in the goods shed. The lower right siding terminates in the Southampton Corporation's electricity works and was in use until 1964.

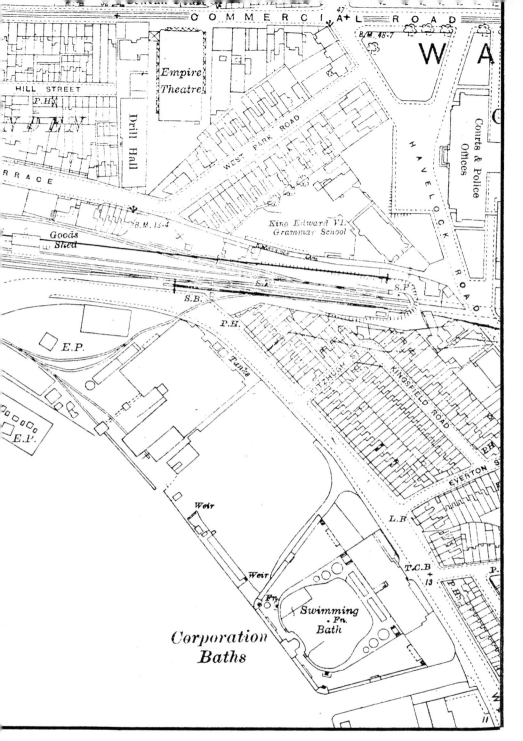

114. Looking east from the public footbridge, one can see Southampton Tunnel, the goods yard and the platforms of the disused first station. The headcode is Waterloo - Bournemouth Special. (Lens of Sutton)

115. Class L12 4-4-0 no. E418 runs into the up platform on 10th November 1928. At that time, the sea lapped the boundary fence on the left at high tide. (H.C.Casserley)

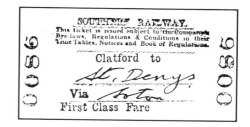

117. The last locomotive to be built at Brighton, class 4 no. 80154, departs with the 9.40am Brighton to Bournemouth West service on 3rd August 1957. This was one of the longest tank engine workings of all time. (D.Fereday Glenn)

116. The 1934 span of the public footbridge is on the left of this picture taken on 21st May 1957. Class T9 no. 30730 is bound for Portsmouth & Southsea, while no. 34012 *Launceston* waits to leave for Waterloo. (H.C.Casserley)

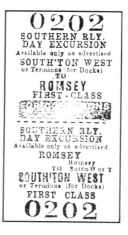

118. The suffix "Central" was in use between 7th July 1935 and 10th July 1967, although it was still on the box when photographed on 16th September 1970. The up side of the station was completely rebuilt in 1968, when a five storey office block was erected. (J.Scrace)

ANDOVER, ROMSEY, & SOUTHAMPTON.—L. & S.W.

Miles from Andover J.	Waterloo Bridge, LONDON 32 dep	mrn	mrn 1050	aft 3 50
	From Salisbury, see page 35.	1,2,3 mrn	1,2,3 aft	1,2,3 aft
	Andover Junc. dp	7 30	1240	6 5
½	,, Town..	7 31	1250	6 9
2	Clatford	7 40	1 1	6 15
5½	Fullerton Bridge..	7 49	1 16	6 24
8½	Stockbridge	7 58	1 31	6 34
11½	Horsebridge......	8 7	1 45	6 43
14½	Mottisfont	8 14	1 54	6 51
18	Romsey 38, 34..	8 22	2 8	7 0
23½	Redbridge 33....	8 37	2 30	7 15
25½	Millbrook ....[34	8 41	2 36	7 20
—	S'hmptn (W. End)	8 44	2 39	7 23
28	.. Docks Sta.ar	8 53	2 46	7 33

Fm Dorchstr, p. 34	1,2,3	1,2,3	1,2,3
Docks Station, Southampton dp	mrn 9 30	aft 3 30	aft 7 55
,, West End	9 37	3 35	8 2
Millbrook........	9 41	3 39	8 5
Redbridge	9 56	3 43	8 9
Romsey .... 34, 38 arr	1011	3 55	8 21
Romsey .... 34, 38 dep	1020	3 56	8 22
Mottisfont	1031	4 5	8 29
Horsebridge......	1045	4 13	8 35
Stockbridge......	11 4	4 21	8 43
Fullerton Bridge.	1117	4 31	8 53
Clatford	1130	4 39	9 0
Andover Town ..	1136	4 46	9 7
,, Junc.35,32a	115	4 50	9 11
LONDON 35 arr	2 13	6 53	....

No Sunday Trains.

June 1869

For other photographs and maps of the Redbridge - Southampton line, please see our *Southampton to Bournemouth* album. Southampton Terminus is included in our *Woking to Southampton* and *Portsmouth to Southampton* albums, while other photographs of the entire route are to be found in Peter Hay's *Steaming Through West Hants*. Further details of the canal that preceded the line are available in *Hampshire Waterways* by P.A.L.Vine. All these book are published by Middleton Press.

←

119. Colour light signalling was introduced on 8th November 1981, since when control has been from Eastleigh Panel. No. 31149 accelerates the Portsmouth Harbour - Bristol Temple Meads service away from the station on 21st August 1982. At that time, class 31s only appeared twice on Saturdays. The 1934 bridge is in the background. (J.S.Petley)

120. Millbrook is in the distance as two Sprinter units approach Southampton on 6th August 1988, forming the 05.47 Milford Haven to Brighton service. Introduced to the route in May of that year, these units sadly have leg room for those under 5ft tall with windows positioned for those over 6ft. However , their performance lives up to their fleet name. (P.G.Barnes)

MP Middleton Press

Easebourne Lane, Midhurst. West Sussex. GU29 9AZ
(0730) 813169

Write or telephone for our latest booklist

BRANCH LINES

BRANCH LINES TO MIDHURST
BRANCH LINES AROUND MIDHURST
BRANCH LINES TO HORSHAM
BRANCH LINES TO EAST GRINSTEAD
BRANCH LINES TO ALTON
BRANCH LINE TO HAYLING
BRANCH LINE TO TENTERDEN
BRANCH LINES TO NEWPORT
BRANCH LINES TO TUNBRIDGE WELLS
BRANCH LINE TO SWANAGE
BRANCH LINES TO LONGMOOR
BRANCH LINE TO LYME REGIS
BRANCH LINE TO FAIRFORD
BRANCH LINE TO ALLHALLOWS
BRANCH LINES AROUND ASCOT
BRANCH LINES AROUND WEYMOUTH
BRANCH LINE TO HAWKHURST
BRANCH LINES AROUND EFFINGHAM JN
BRANCH LINE TO MINEHEAD

SOUTH COAST RAILWAYS

CHICHESTER TO PORTSMOUTH
BRIGHTON TO EASTBOURNE
RYDE TO VENTNOR
EASTBOURNE TO HASTINGS
PORTSMOUTH TO SOUTHAMPTON
HASTINGS TO ASHFORD
SOUTHAMPTON TO BOURNEMOUTH
ASHFORD TO DOVER
BOURNEMOUTH TO WEYMOUTH
DOVER TO RAMSGATE

SOUTHERN MAIN LINES

HAYWARDS HEATH TO SEAFORD
EPSOM TO HORSHAM
CRAWLEY TO LITTLEHAMPTON
THREE BRIDGES TO BRIGHTON
WATERLOO TO WOKING
VICTORIA TO EAST CROYDON
TONBRIDGE TO HASTINGS
EAST CROYDON TO THREE BRIDGES
WOKING TO SOUTHAMPTON
WATERLOO TO WINDSOR
LONDON BRIDGE TO EAST CROYDON

COUNTRY RAILWAY ROUTES

BOURNEMOUTH TO EVERCREECH JN
READING TO GUILDFORD
WOKING TO ALTON
BATH TO EVERCREECH JUNCTION
GUILDFORD TO REDHILL
EAST KENT LIGHT RAILWAY
FAREHAM TO SALISBURY
BURNHAM TO EVERCREECH JUNCTION
REDHILL TO ASHFORD
YEOVIL TO DORCHESTER
ANDOVER TO SOUTHAMPTON

LONDON SUBURBAN RAILWAYS

CHARING CROSS TO DARTFORD
HOLBORN VIADUCT TO LEWISHAM
KINGSTON & HOUNSLOW LOOPS

STEAMING THROUGH

STEAMING THROUGH EAST HANTS
STEAMING THROUGH SURREY
STEAMING THROUGH WEST SUSSEX
STEAMING THROUGH THE ISLE OF WIGHT
STEAMING THROUGH WEST HANTS

OTHER RAILWAY BOOKS

GARRAWAY FATHER & SON
LONDON CHATHAM & DOVER RAILWAY
INDUSTRIAL RAILWAYS OF THE S. EAST
WEST SUSSEX RAILWAYS IN THE 1980s
SOUTH EASTERN RAILWAY - due late 1990

OTHER BOOKS

MIDHURST TOWN THEN & NOW
EAST GRINSTEAD THEN & NOW

WALKS IN THE WESTERN HIGH WEALD
TILLINGBOURNE BUS STORY

MILITARY DEFENCE OF WEST SUSSEX
BATTLE OVER SUSSEX 1940

SURREY WATERWAYS
KENT AND EAST SUSSEX WATERWAYS
HAMPSHIRE WATERWAYS